The Blessing of Obedience

by
Norvel Hayes

HARRISON HOUSE
Tulsa, Oklahoma

All Scripture quotations are taken from the *King James Version* of the Bible.

16 15 14 13 12   27 26 25 24

The Blessing of Obedience
ISBN-13: 978-0-89274-355-1
ISBN-10: 0-89274-355-7
Copyright © 1982 by Norvel Hayes
P.O. Box 1379
Cleveland, TN 37311

Published by Harrison House, Inc.
P. O. Box 35035
Tulsa, Oklahoma 74153

The Blessing of Obedience

In those days came John the Baptist, preaching in the wilderness of Judaea, and saying, Repent ye: for the kingdom of heaven is at hand. For this is he that was spoken of by the prophet Esaias, saying, The Voice of one crying in the wilderness, Prepare ye the way of the Lord, make his paths straight.

And the same John had his raiment of camel's hair, and a leathern girdle about his loins; and his meat was locusts and wild honey.

Then went out to him Jerusalem, and all Judaea, and all the region round about Jordan, and were baptized of him in Jordan, confessing their sins.

But when he saw many of the Pharisees and Sadducees come to his baptism, he said unto them, O generation of vipers, who hath warned you to flee from the wrath to come? Bring forth therefore fruits meet for repentance.

Matthew 3:1-8

When was the last time you won a soul? When was the last time you gave something to a needy person? When was the last time you took God's healing power to the sick?

Pause for a moment and ask yourself these questions. When was the last time you — not somebody else, but *you*—brought forth fruit to the Lord? If you're trying to live a Christian life without bringing fruit to Jesus, you are a rebellious child of God. You are cutting yourself off from the many blessings God has for you.

God likes busy men and busy women. An idle mind is the devil's workshop. If you'll worship God, read the Bible, pray in tongues, win souls, pray for the sick, and cast out devils, you'll never go crazy.

If you'll be willing to obey God, He will keep you so busy that demons can't catch you.

They won't have a chance to get into your mind. devils can't get in your mind anyway unless you think about them. You have to first think about the temptations they offer you, and then begin to yield to them.

The Bible says that in order to work for God and not be rebellious, you have to keep your flesh under subjection. It is the nature of the flesh to rebel against the things of God.

Confusion Causes Rebellion

Until I was baptized in the Holy Ghost, I didn't fully understand some things.

I was raised in the Baptist Church, and we didn't believe in healing, casting out devils, speaking in tongues, or operating in the gifts of the Spirit. A person could get saved or born again there; but it was foolish to take a cancer patient to our church to get healed.

You may ask, "Why don t churches like that get people healed?" Because they haven't received the truth of Mark 11:24 and James 5:14; they are still doubting and wondering.

As long as you are a rebel against a particular portion of the Bible, God won't work for you in that area.

My Baptist mother died of cancer at 37 years of age. My brother, a football player in high school, died at 19 of Bright's disease. Nobody ever told them that Jesus was a healer.

Most of the people we knew were ashamed of it. All of us boys in the First Baptist church were ashamed. We wouldn't have been caught dead in a tent meeting that said, "Healing Crusade." We didn't know that the preacher under the tent was perhaps the only one in town to have the truth.

There we were making five thousand dollars a week, wearing our tailor-made suits, riding in Cadillacs, and going to the First church, saying, "We've got it. Those other people are just wild. We ought to feel sorry for them."

To be truthful, we were more confused than the devil because even the devil knows Jesus will heal people. (It's awful to be more stupid than the devil!)

4

We were in rebellion against God and the Bible. If you want to know what God is like, read the Bible. Jesus said, *Lay hands on the sick, and they shall recover* (Mark 16:18).

God sent me to a Full Gospel church there in Cleveland, Tennessee, to train me; but I was so rebellious that I was ashamed to go inside. I would look both ways to see if any of the First Baptist boys were watching. I knew — God wanted me there, but I didn't want any of my relatives and friends to see me going in.

Bring Fruits to God

We have to learn not to be rebellious against God. People could prevent much of this rebellion if they would learn to bring fruit to God.

Don't be concerned about what the other fellow is doing; be concerned first about what you are doing for God. You must reach the point that you are willing to put your own desires aside and do what God wants you to do. When you cross that line, God will bless you. You will be in the place for God to give you His peace 24 hours a day, 365 days a year.

I am never confused about anything. I haven't had a confused day in years. I have the peace of God in me all the time — 24 hours a day, 365 days a year. I don't believe in sad days.

Now I didn't say that the devil doesn't try to visit me; but when he does, I just say, "In Jesus' name, go from me!" Then I begin to worship the Lord. I say, "Oh Jesus, I worship You and praise You." Every morning when I open my eyes, I say several times, "I love You, Jesus." Then I try to spend some time just worshiping Him. When I do, His warm and tender presence just comes on me.

Next, I begin to confess who I am in Christ Jesus. I confess that I am not a rebel against God. I say, "The Bible says in 1 Samuel 15:23 that rebellion is the same as witchcraft. I am not a rebel against God." Then I confess that I will do what God wants me to do.

6

Some people say, "It's so hard to live the Christian life." But if you present yourself to God like this, you will find that it's the easiest thing you ever tried. Don't be a rebel against the Bible, God, Jesus, and the Holy Ghost. When the Holy Ghost tells you to do something, do it!

One time the Holy Ghost told me to park my car in front of a parsonage and start praying in tongues. I lay down in the front seat and began to cry and make intercession for the pastor's daughter, who was considering marrying the wrong person.

The Holy Ghost knows exactly what He is doing. After I had been there about an hour, praying in tongues, the Spirit of God suddenly came upon the daughter in the house and she began to scream. She ran outside and jumped in my car, shouting, "I don't want to give him up! I don't want to give him up! Do I have to give him up?"

I said, "Yes, you have to give him up."

She replied, "But it's not easy to give up somebody like that."

7

Obedience Produces Fruit

Obeying the Holy Ghost, then, involves bringing forth fruits. John the Baptist said, **Bring forth therefore fruits meet for repentance: and think not to say within yourselves, We have Abraham to our father: for I say unto you, that God is able of these stones to raise up children unto Abraham** (Matt. 3:8,9).

The average person will say, "I'm okay; I belong to such-and-such church." A national survey says that over 95 percent of the Christians in America have never won a soul and that over 60 percent of the born-again Christians in our country learned the foundation of the new birth through a book or a tract.

No wonder God told me several years ago to sow seeds on college campuses by giving out books and tracts. I have given out books and tracts by the hundreds of thousands from the University of Maine to the University of California. At first I could hardly believe that God wanted me to do it; I was already so busy. But I didn't question it.

God spoke to me as I was sitting in a sorority house at the University of Florida. About 85 girls in the dining room began to sing a dirty song. (I was the only man in the house.) I dropped my head and began to pray. I said, "Help these girls, Jesus. Get to these students."

I had been praying for about five minutes when the Spirit of God came on me and said, "I will if *you* will; but I *can't* if you *don't!*" Jesus wanted to walk into that sorority house and save every girl, but He couldn't. The Gospel is spread through men. The Gospel is spread through *you*, and it won't get spread if you are a rebellious child.

Beware of rebellion against God!

Not too long after that, I told God I would begin a campus ministry. I continued to tell Him that for about three months, but I never did anything about it. Then I was in Memphis holding a meeting for several hundred young people. Someone walked up to me and said, "God told me to give you a motor home." Another person put a $100 bill in my pocket. Then three fraternity boys from Memphis

9

State walked up and said, "While you were speaking, Jesus told us to start working for you, handing out tracts and books."

I thought, "Dear Lord! A man has given me a motor home; another fellow hands me a $100 bill to buy some tracts; and three boys come up and say, 'Here we are.'"

Then the Lord said to me, "Get it?"

For the next three years I had four or five witnessing teams covering college campuses across the country. Finally, I said, "Well, I've covered the country four or five times now. I guess I can let this ministry drop off to the side."

At this time I was in Nashville with Reverend Kenneth Hagin and his wife, Oretha. As I was getting ready to go back home, they said, "Norvel, the Lord wants us to pray before you leave." The moment we began to pray, the Spirit of God hit Brother Hagin. He started to cry and say, "Precious, precious, precious is the ministry to the young people. Precious is the ministry to the college kids."

Needless to say, God got through to me; and I repented. *God* had never told me to stop; *I* had said I was going to stop. But God never wants you to stop until *He* says so.

Don't rebel against God. If He tells you to do something, go ahead, even if it looks so big you think you can't do it. You'll be able to if you start out slow and start out small. The Holy Ghost will help you.

Can God Trust You?

God only helps and promotes those He can trust. The Spirit of God will help you if He can trust you. If He has never helped you do anything, then He can't trust you.

The same is true with the gifts of the Spirit. The Holy Ghost will give you the gifts as you minister. They will flow through you as the Spirit wills if He can trust you with them.

Ask yourself right now, "Can Jesus trust me to worship Him and to bring forth fruit unto Him?"

It isn't enough to say, "I belong to the Methodist church or the Pentecostal church." You can't just say, "I've been a church member for twenty-five years." It isn't enough to join a nice church in your community, go there every Sunday, and get mad if you don t have a good, spiritual service.

When are you going to sow seed yourself? Have you ever brought a sinner to church? God wants you to win souls yourself. Sure, you need a spiritual church where you can learn to worship God and work; but God wants you to bring forth fruit unto Him, and you will never bring it forth as long as you are a rebel against God and His Word.

Be Delivered From Yourself

If you're not bringing forth good fruit to Jesus, you need to be delivered from yourself.

One time when I was asked to minister God's Word at a large university, I was given a meeting room for a week. In one of the meetings an alcoholic was delivered and later

12

brought the university psychiatrist. The psychiatrist sat and listened; then after the service he said to me, "I want to make an appointment to talk with you when you are available."

I said, "Okay. We'll talk this afternoon."

As we talked together, he said, "I've never before heard anybody like you, and I've never sat for three hours without smoking a cigarette. I guess you know that my mind is telling me what you're saying isn't true."

I said, "I know your mind is telling you that; but, Doctor, I can help you if you'll let me. Just pull that intellectual mind out of your head, lay it aside, and come to God as a little child. Say, 'God, I'm dumb; but I'm willing for You to teach me. Teach me Your ways, Lord. Show me Your reality.'"

Then the Holy Ghost began to show me something about him. I said, "All day you tell people how to live. Then you go to the country club every afternoon and sit with your friends, drinking and telling dirty jokes. How many times have you sat there after

13

telling people how to live all day long and not even known how to live yourself? How often have you said, 'Is this all life has to offer?'"

"Oh, I've said that a lot of times. How did you know?"

"Doctor, God will give you a brand new life. You don't know anything about God – you're a rebel against Him — but if you'll let me, I'll teach you enough to find Him. Come to class tonight."

That night I spoke on "God's Double Dose." I talked about being baptized in the Holy Ghost, speaking in other tongues, and being healed. When I got through, I gave an invitation for healing. The moment I gave it, the psychiatrist jumped out of his seat, came down in front of the whole class, and stood there. He was ready to receive from God!

The first thing you must do in order to receive from God is to get delivered from yourself. Like the psychiatrist, you have to forget about the people around you and put your pride aside. You have to be delivered from yourself — not somebody else, *yourself*.

Use What God Gives You

Suppose a radio pastor suddenly said, "Well, God, I think I'm going to cancel about 450 radio stations and speak once every three months. I've got enough money to get a place in Florida, so I'm just going to take it easy for a while. But I love You, Lord!"

After about three months, the things God had blessed him with would begin to drop off. Why? Because he wasn't using them. You have to use what God gives you. If you don't, it will get stale.

Jesus gave us the Great Commission, and He expects us to use it. He said:

Go ye into all the world, and preach the gospel to every creature . . .

And these signs shall follow them that believe; In my name shall they cast out devils; they shall speak with new tongues;

They shall take up serpents; and if they drink any deadly thing, it shall not hurt them; they shall lay hands on the sick, and they shall recover.

Mark 16:15,17,18

Don't be rebellious against God. Do what He has told you to do. Cast out devils when you come upon them. (But don't look for a devil behind every tree; devils aren't in everybody.) When you come upon a sick person, lay your hands on him.

Recently while speaking in Atlanta, Georgia, I gave an invitation, and a man stumbled to the front. You could tell he was a wino; he was filthy and the smell was almost unbearable.

He looked up at me and said, "The church I went to threw me out three times; but something told me that if I came here tonight, you wouldn't throw me out."

I replied, "That's right. You won't get thrown out of here. Come here."

I put my arms around him, and the Spirit of the Lord began to come upon him.

You might ask, "How could you put your arms around someone so filthy and dirty?"

God has delivered me from tailor-made suits and Cadillacs. I still have some of these things, but I have been delivered from them.

(It's all right to have things as long as you're delivered from them — as long as they don't have you!)

It was nothing for me to put my arms around that man and say, "We love you. Get on your knees right now, and we'll pray for you. It doesn't make any difference how many bottles of whiskey you've drunk, we'll get hold of God for you and you won't be drinking anymore. When God comes, the whiskey goes."

Today, that person doesn't even look the same. He goes to that church and wears clean clothes now.

Jesus has never turned against lonely, hopeless drunks, and He never will. But He has to work through you. God wants good fruit.

Ministering In The City Dump

Years ago, I got delivered from myself at the city dump. I had seen that God was going to use me and thought He had made a mistake. For three or four years, I tried to talk

Him out of it. Every night He would come into my room. I would get out of bed and cry, "God, You don't want me; I'm no good. I've never done anything for You. I'm not a preacher. You don't want me, Lord."

But He acted like He had no ears. He would say to me, "Come, follow Me, and believe the Bible."

When I saw that He wasn't going to give up, and that He loved me enough to come into my room every night, I made up my mind to follow Him and do what He wanted me to do.

I said, "God, I don't have any sense, so You'll have to train me." I thought He would send me to a church or to a big auditorium; instead He sent me to the city dump! The houses there were pitiful; the people who lived there were in bad shape. They smelled so bad that I had to hold my nose to pray for them.

I never will forget the time I prayed for a woman while bugs were crawling on the bed with her. It isn't nice to stand beside somebody's bed and try to pray while the bugs are crawling out!

After I finished praying for her, I walked across the street to a house that must have had 40,000 flies inside! A woman lived there with her three children.

A little girl walked over to me and said, "Mister, this is all the milk the baby has, and we don't have any food. We don't have anything."

I walked outside and said, "God, is this what I get for leaving my church?" It was a Bible course straight from heaven! When I said that, God overshadowed me and I broke down. I will never forget it as long as I live.

He said, "Son, be faithful to Me here and I'll promote you."

"Yes, Lord."

"They need some milk in the house. What are you going to do about it?"

"Well, Lord, I'm going to the store and buy some milk and food."

"Show Me. Talk is cheap."

God is always wanting you to show Him

something. Until you start doing something, you are a rebel against God.

Again, I quote John the Baptist: **And now also the axe is laid unto the root of the trees: therefore every tree which bringeth not forth good fruit is hewn down, and cast into the fire** (Matt. 3:10). By showing God something, you are bringing forth good fruit.

My Will Vs. God's Will

Several years ago God taught me a lesson. I thought that when I became born-again and Spirit-filled, I could do whatever I wanted to do. I wasn't interested in bringing forth good fruit to God the way I should have been.

One weekend I made up my mind to drive from Cleveland, Tennessee, to Augusta, Georgia; stay there for two days visiting; leave Augusta Saturday morning; go to the University of Georgia campus; watch Tennessee beat Georgia; then drive home after the ball game.

That was how I planned to spend my weekend, and nothing was going to interfere with it.

While in Augusta, a Full Gospel pastor said to me, "Brother Norvel, the Lord told me He wants you to speak at my church Sunday morning." I didn't know what the Lord had told him because I hadn't listened to the Lord myself.

If you make plans without praying, you'll miss God every time. Don't do it. You'll be in rebellion against God. Once you make up your mind, God can't reach you.

God will let you do all kinds of things that you shouldn't do. If you don't go to him in prayer and learn to be led by the inward witness, you will end up making a lot of mistakes.

If you feel in your spirit that you shouldn't do something, then don't do it. If you feel good about it — like velvet on the inside — that's the signal from the Holy Ghost to go ahead. The Spirit of God is here to help you and He will — if you pray and let Him lead you.

I hadn't prayed about my plans for the weekend. I just said, "I'm going to the ball game Saturday. I've already made up my mind."

When the pastor invited me to speak, I made up an excuse and said, "I'll come back and speak for you some other time."

The pastor had said he wanted to see me; so Saturday morning on my way out of town I stopped by his house. He had gone to the church, and I was sitting in his living room with some other people. Suddenly I began to feel pain around my heart. Then the pastor telephoned to say that the church janitor had just had a heart attack. Immediately we went into prayer.

In a few minutes he called back to report that the janitor had died. He asked, "Would you go with me to tell his wife? They own a store in town."

"Yes, I'll go."

So we went to the store and talked with his wife. All this time I was still planning to go to the Tennessee/Georgia game.

While I was standing there in that store, the Spirit of God hit me like a bolt of lightning. The Lord said, "Go to the church and pray." The assistant pastor was standing there, so I told him what the Lord had said.

As I entered the church and was walking toward the pulpit, the Holy Spirit moved on me and I fell to my knees in prayer. I didn't know it, but the Spirit of God was making intercession for me. *For me!*

After I had prayed for about twenty minutes in the Spirit (in tongues), the Holy Ghost began to groan through me. I was lying flat on the floor in front of the pulpit, groaning. The Spirit of God had taken me to the point that all I could do was groan. For nearly three hours I lay there groaning before God. I couldn't get up.

After that time (just when Tennessee was beating Georgia!), I pushed myself up to a sitting position and said, 'All right, Lord, I'll speak at this church Sunday morning."

The Baptism of Fire

John the Baptist said:

I indeed baptize you with water unto repentance; but he that cometh after me is mightier than I, whose shoes I am not worthy to bear; he shall baptize you with the Holy Ghost, and with fire.

Matthew 3:11

There are three baptisms: water, the Holy Ghost, and fire. Nearly everyone believes in water baptism; many have experienced Holy Ghost baptism; but only a small number have been baptized in the fire of God.

As long as you leave off the fire, you will stay in some degree of rebellion as a child of God. But if you will spend time praying in the Spirit and yield yourself to Him — to the Greater One Who lives inside you — He will burn *you* out of you. (So many people want to do what *they* want to do, the way *they* want to do it.)

At that point in my life, I needed to be baptized in fire. I stayed in Augusta and spoke Sunday morning. The altar call lasted more than an hour. Fifteen or twenty people were baptized in the Holy Ghost, and many were saved. They flooded the altar.

Finally, we went to lunch about two o'clock. Again, I was planning to leave. As we were sitting there, I said, "As soon as we finish eating, I'm going back to get my clothes because I'm going home this afternoon."

But the pastor replied, "Oh, no, you're not! I'm going to get a revival out of this."

"A revival! No, pastor, be quiet!"

He repeated, "I'm going to get a revival out of this. You're not going anywhere!"

But I insisted, "I am going home. I want to go this afternoon."

After that, I seemed to get weaker with every bit of food. I had to be helped into the car and into the parsonage. I went to sleep and woke up at 5:30, feeling refreshed; in fact, I felt like a teenager! I was ready to go; but by then it was too late to go home, so I decided, "I might as well stay and speak again tonight."

Burning Out the Chaff

What happened to me that weekend? In Matthew 3:12 John the Baptist is describing Jesus, the coming Messiah. He says:

Whose fan is in his hand, and he will thoroughly purge his floor, and gather his wheat into the garner; but he will burn up the chaff with unquenchable fire.

God was burning the chaff out of me. The fire of God was burning *Norvel Hayes* out of Norvel Hayes. He was burning out that overwhelming desire for football games. (I still like football, but I'm usually too busy to go to games.) There is nothing wrong with football as long as you don't put it before God. I'm warning you: unless you want to wind up on the floor, groaning for three hours, don't put football games before God! He is no respecter of persons, and I've already been there, so take my advice.

Prayer Is the Key

Jesus was a Man of prayer. He would spend hour after hour in prayer before the Father God.

One year when I was a speaker at the Full Gospel Business Men's convention in Jerusalem, I stood in the Garden of Gethsemane where Jesus prayed until His sweat turned to blood. As I was standing there, His presence came upon me; it was a sweet experience!

Take my word for it, there is power in prayer. It makes you feel good to know that if you stay before God, you'll get some answers.

You can't defeat a person who prays. The storms may come, but he will just keep on praying until he prays himself out of them. He says:

"In Jesus' name, I will not take a storm from the devil. I belong to Jesus. I will not be rebellious; I will pray myself out of the storm."

Above all, you need to pray in tongues. To know the will of God, you need to pray in the Spirit continually. As you do, you will be walking in God's power.

The Bible says God's power is a way of life. That doesn't mean to worship God on Sunday, then go your own way on Monday,

Tuesday, Wednesday, Thursday, Friday and Saturday.

If you are not spending time in prayer and worship before God, you need to be delivered from yourself. Until you are delivered from yourself, you won't bring forth good fruit.

Ask God in prayer to deliver you from yourself. As you begin to yield to the direction of the Holy Ghost, that element of rebellion will be removed from your life. The Lord Jesus Christ will be pleased with you, and God's power will become a way of living.

For a complete list of tapes and books
by Norvel Hayes, write:
Norvel Hayes
P O. Box 1379
Cleveland, TN 37311
Feel free to include your prayer requests and comments when you write.

About the Author

Norvel Hayes is a successful businessman, internationally renowned Bible teacher, and founder of several Christian ministries in the U.S. and abroad.

Brother Hayes founded *New Life Bible College,* located in Cleveland, Tennessee, in 1977. *New Life Bible Church* grew out of the Bible school's chapel services. The Bible School offers a two-year diploma and off-campus correspondence courses. Among it's many other out-reaches, the church ministers God's Word and hot meals daily to the poor through the *New Life Soup Kitchen.*

Brother Hayes is also the founder and president of *New Life Maternity Home,* a ministry dedicated to the spiritual, physical and financial need of young girls during pregnancy; *Campus Challenge,* and evangelistic outreach that distributes Christian literature on college campuses across America; *Street Reach,* a ministry dedicated to runaway teens located in Daytona Beach, Florida; and *Children's Home,* an orphanage home and education center located in India.

Known internationally for his dynamic exposition of the Word of God, Brother Hayes spends most of his time teaching and ministering God's deliverance and healing power in churches, college classrooms, conventions and seminars around the world.

Books by Norvel Hayes

Don't Let the Devil Steal Your Destiny

How to Live and Not Die

Worship

The Blessing of Obedience

The Chosen Fast

Confession Brings Possession

How To Get Your Prayers Answered

Let Not Your Heart Be Troubled

Misguided Faith

The Number One Way To Fight the Devil

What To Do for Healing

Available from your local bookstore.
HARRISON HOUSE
P.O. Box 35035
Tulsa, OK 74153

The Harrison House Vision
Proclaiming the truth and the power
Of the Gospel of Jesus Christ
With excellence;

Challenging Christians to
Live victoriously,
Grow spiritually,
Know God intimately.